Autism Without Limits

A Comprehensive Guide to Understanding Behaviors and Supporting Positive Growth

Copyright © 2024

No part of this publication may be reproduced, stored in a retrieval system, or transmitted in any form or by any means, electronic, mechanical, photocopying, recording, or otherwise, without the prior written permission of the publisher.

Printed in the United States of America

First Edition: 2024

This copyright page includes the necessary copyright notice, permissions request information, acknowledgments for the cover design, interior design, and editing, as well as the details of the first edition.

Disclaimer: This book is a work of non-fiction and is intended solely for informational and educational purposes. The names mentioned within are trademarks of their respective owners. This publication is not affiliated with, endorsed by, or sponsored by any of these trademark holders. The inclusion of these names is meant to provide context and historical reference.

The author does not claim ownership of any trademarks or copyrights related to the names and likenesses of the individuals referenced in this book. Any opinions expressed herein are those of the author and do not necessarily reflect the views of any organization or trademark holder.

Introduction

In a world that can feel like a whirlwind, where miscommunication and social hiccups often create rifts, navigating Autism Spectrum Disorder (ASD) is a journey that's both unique and profound. Every person on the spectrum has their own story—full of potential and hurdles—but too often, these narratives get lost in a sea of myths and misunderstandings. This book aims to shine a light on the intricacies of autism, offering insights that promote understanding, compassion, and growth.

Getting a grip on autism isn't just a dry academic exercise; it's a deeply personal journey that resonates with families, teachers, and communities. Once a diagnosis hits, a flood of questions can come crashing in: What does this mean for my kid? How can I help them grow? What resources are out there to guide us through this maze? This guide is here to equip readers with the knowledge and practical tips needed to support individuals with autism in reaching their full potential.

Digging into the science of autism reveals a rich tapestry of neurological differences, genetic factors, and environmental impacts. It makes us think about how these elements influence behavior, communication, and social interactions. By grasping the nuances of sensory processing, we can start to see the world through the eyes of those on the spectrum—realizing that what looks like challenging behavior is often just a different way of expressing themselves, craving understanding.

Communication is key to connecting with others, but it can be a tough nut to crack for many with autism. This book dives into various communication styles and shares effective strategies to bridge the gap between expression and understanding. Tools like visual supports, social stories, and customized approaches help individuals share their thoughts and feelings, building meaningful relationships along the way.

As we flip through the pages, we'll also highlight the critical role of developing social skills. Figuring out social cues can feel like climbing a mountain, but with the right techniques and a supportive environment, individuals with autism can make friends and thrive socially. This guide champions inclusion and peer relationships, pushing for a world where everyone feels valued and accepted.

But wait, there's more! The journey goes beyond just communication and social skills; it digs into emotional regulation and mental health too. Anxiety, depression, and emotional ups and downs are real challenges. By giving individuals the tools they need for emotional well-being, we can help them navigate their inner worlds, building resilience and self-advocacy.

In the education arena, this book stresses the importance of personalized approaches, teamwork between families and educators, and the magic of tailored learning experiences. It highlights fostering independence, teaching life skills, and prepping individuals for life's transitions. Each chapter acts as a stepping stone toward empowerment, showing that the autism journey isn't a solo trek but a shared adventure.

Throughout this guide, we celebrate the strengths and talents that individuals with autism bring to the table. Their unique viewpoints and skills enrich our communities and challenge the traditional ideas of success. By sharing uplifting stories and recognizing individual talents, we spark hope and open doors for everyone.

As we work to build a supportive community, we can't overlook the importance of advocacy and awareness in fostering acceptance. By raising our voices and promoting understanding, we can break down stigma and create a more inclusive society. Together, we can craft spaces where individuals with autism are celebrated for who they are, not just labeled by their challenges.

This book invites you on a transformative journey—one that aims to break down barriers, nurture understanding, and create a sense of belonging for individuals with autism and their families. It's a rallying cry for educators, caregivers, advocates, and anyone willing to embrace the beauty of neurodiversity. Together, we can push for a future where autism is understood without limits, where everyone gets the chance to thrive, and where the richness of human experience is embraced in all its forms. Welcome aboard this journey of discovery, compassion, and empowerment!

Table of Contents

- Creating sensory-friendly environments

Chapter 7: Educational Approaches and Strategies
- Individualized Education Plans (IEPs) and their components
- Effective teaching methods for diverse learning styles
- The role of collaboration between educators and families

Chapter 8: Family Dynamics and Support
- Navigating family relationships and dynamics
- Resources and support networks for families
- Self-care strategies for caregivers

Chapter 9: Fostering Independence
- Teaching daily living skills and routines
- The importance of choice and autonomy
- Preparing for transitions into adulthood

Chapter 10: Emotional Regulation and Mental Health
- Understanding emotional dysregulation in autism
- Techniques for promoting emotional well-being
- The impact of anxiety and depression on individuals with autism

Chapter 11: Therapeutic Interventions
- Overview of various therapies (ABA, OT, Speech)
- Choosing the right therapy for individual needs
- Measuring the effectiveness of therapeutic interventions

Chapter 12: The Role of Technology
- Assistive technology and communication devices
- Apps and tools for social skills and learning
- The potential of virtual reality in therapy

Chapter 1

Understanding Autism Spectrum Disorder

Autism Spectrum Disorder (ASD) is like a vast ocean—deep, complex, and filled with a myriad of unique characteristics. When we discuss the autism spectrum, we're not just tossing around a label; we're diving into a rich tapestry of behaviors, strengths, and challenges. Imagine a colorful spectrum, much like a rainbow, where each hue represents a different experience, a different way of interacting with the world.

So, what exactly is ASD? It's a developmental disorder that affects how individuals communicate, interact, and perceive their surroundings. It's not a one-size-fits-all situation. Some individuals might be non-verbal, while others boast an expansive vocabulary. Some may struggle with social cues, while others thrive in structured environments. The characteristics of autism can range from challenges in social interactions and communication to repetitive behaviors and intense focus on specific interests. Think of it as a unique operating system; it's not broken, just different.

Now, let's address some common myths and misconceptions about autism. First off, let's clear the air: Autism is NOT a disease. It's not something you catch like a cold or something that can be "fixed." It's a lifelong condition that shapes how a person interacts with the world. One of the biggest misconceptions is that all individuals with autism lack empathy. That's simply not true! Many individuals on the spectrum feel emotions deeply but may express them differently. Just because someone doesn't react in the way you expect doesn't mean they don't care.

Another myth that needs busting is the idea that autism is solely a childhood disorder. Newsflash: Autism doesn't magically disappear when you hit adulthood. In fact, many adults on the spectrum face unique challenges that can often go unnoticed. So, if you think you've got it all figured out because you've read a few articles, think again.

Now, let's talk about early diagnosis and intervention. Why is it so crucial? Well, let me share a little story. A few years back, I met a family whose son was diagnosed with autism at the age of two. They jumped into early intervention services, and let me tell you, it was like watching a flower bloom. With the right support, he developed communication skills, social interactions, and a love for learning. On the flip side, I've seen families who waited until their kids were in school to seek help. The difference was night and day.

Research shows that early intervention can significantly improve outcomes for children with autism. The earlier a child receives support, the better their chances are for developing essential skills. According to the CDC, early diagnosis can lead to better educational and social outcomes. So, if you suspect something's off, don't hesitate. Trust your instincts and seek professional advice.

Here's a quick rundown of the importance of early diagnosis and intervention:

1. Enhanced Developmental Outcomes: Early intervention can help improve communication, social skills, and cognitive abilities.

2. Tailored Support: Professionals can create individualized plans that cater to the child's unique needs, leading to more effective strategies.

3. Family Support: Early diagnosis opens doors to resources and support networks for families, making the journey less isolating.

4. Long-term Benefits: Studies show that children who receive early intervention often require fewer services later in life.

But here's the kicker: even if you missed the early window, it's never too late to seek help. There are plenty of resources available for individuals of all ages. The key is to stay informed and proactive.

Now, let's get real for a second. Understanding autism isn't just about knowing the facts; it's about fostering empathy and connection. If you're a parent, teacher, or just someone who wants to be a better ally, take the time to learn about the spectrum. Talk to individuals with autism, listen to their stories, and understand their perspectives.

To wrap this up, here are a few actionable steps you can take:

- Educate Yourself: Read books, attend workshops, or join online forums. Knowledge is power!

- Engage with the Community: Reach out to local autism organizations or support groups. You'll find a wealth of resources and people who understand the journey.

- Advocate for Early Intervention: If you're a parent, stay vigilant about your child's development. Trust your gut and seek help if needed.

- Challenge Myths: Speak up when you hear misconceptions about autism. Your voice can help change the narrative.

Remember, understanding autism is a journey, not a destination. It's about building bridges, breaking down barriers, and creating a world where everyone can thrive. So, let's dive in, explore the depths of the spectrum, and support one another along the way. After all, we're all in this together, navigating the waters of life, one wave at a time.

Chapter 2

The Lowdown on Autism

Alright, let's jump right into the world of autism. Hang tight, 'cause we're about to unpack the brain, genetics, and sensory stuff. It's a wild ride, and you're gonna come out of this with a fresh outlook.

First up, let's chat about how brains work differently for folks with autism. Think of the brain like a super-complex computer. Instead of running on Windows or macOS, some brains have their own unique OS. So, while everyone thinks, feels, and interacts, the way they do it can be totally different.

Research shows that autistic brains often have different structures and connections. Some studies point to unusual growth patterns in early childhood. Picture a garden where some plants shoot up faster than others. In this case, certain brain areas might grow at their own pace, leading to unique strengths and challenges.

You might be asking, "What's that mean for everyday life?" Well, it means an autistic person might take in info differently. They might be whizzes at pattern recognition or have an incredible memory but can struggle with social cues or get overwhelmed by too much noise. It's like having a superpower but also a weakness that can trip you up.

Now, let's switch gears and talk about the genetics and environment that play a role in autism. Imagine genetics as the cake recipe. You've got your flour, sugar, and eggs, but then there's the oven temp and baking time—those are the environmental factors. Both are key to how that cake turns out.

Studies say genetics are responsible for about 50-80% of autism risk. That's a big slice! Some genes are linked to autism, but it's not just one gene doing all the work. It's more like a tangled web where multiple genes interact with each other and environmental stuff.

Speaking of the environment, things like exposure to certain substances before birth, parental age, and complications during birth can bump up the chances of autism. It's like tossing in a few extra ingredients to that cake mix—sometimes it works, sometimes it flops.

And we can't skip over sensory processing. Ever walked into a loud concert or a busy mall and felt like you were drowning in noise? That's sensory overload. For many autistic folks, sensory processing can be a mixed bag. Some might be super sensitive to sounds, lights, or textures, while others might not notice sensory input at all.

Imagine this: you're at a party, and everyone's chattering. For you, it's a fun buzz. But for someone with autism, that same scene might feel like a swarm of bees buzzing in their ears. It can be a lot to handle and lead to behaviors that seem weird to others.

So, what do we do with all this info? First, understanding these neurological differences, genetic influences, and sensory processing can help us create a better environment for autistic individuals. Here are some tips to keep in mind:

1. **Watch for Sensory Triggers**: If you're around someone on the spectrum, pay attention to the sensory vibes. Loud noises? Bright lights? If it's a lot, think about adjusting the space or offering a quiet spot for a breather.

2. **Keep Communication Open**: Make it easy for folks to share what they need. Ask things like, "What helps you feel chill?" You might get some great insights.

3. **Learn About Autism**: Knowledge is key! The more you know, the better you can support those on the spectrum. Share what you learn to help build a more inclusive community.

4. **Be Patient and Flexible**: Everyone's journey is different. What works for one person might not work for another. Stay open-minded and ready to change things up.

5. **Celebrate Differences**: Instead of seeing autism as a downside, recognize the strengths that come with it. Many autistic individuals have amazing skills in math, art, or music. Let's embrace those talents!

So, what's the bottom line? Autism isn't a simple label. It's a mix of neurological differences, genetic factors, and sensory experiences. By getting to know these elements, we can create a space that encourages growth and understanding for everyone.

Now, let's keep this train rolling. Next up, we'll dig into the communication challenges many autistic individuals face. Trust me, you won't wanna miss it!

Chapter 3

Communication Challenges

Let's jump right into it! Communication challenges can be a real headache, right? Ever tried talking to someone who doesn't speak your language? Frustrating, isn't it? Now, throw in the unique communication styles of folks with autism, and it's like trying to solve a Rubik's Cube with your eyes closed. But hey, don't sweat it! We're here to break it down.

First things first, let's chat about how individuals with autism communicate. Just like no two snowflakes are the same, every person's style is unique. Some might be chatty, while others stick to gestures or facial expressions. And guess what? Some don't use spoken words at all! They might express themselves through art, music, or tech.

So, how do we close this communication gap? One solid approach is to encourage a mix of communication methods. Think of it as a toolbox—if one tool's a bust, grab another! Picture exchange systems or communication devices can really help folks express their needs and feelings. This isn't just a nice touch; it's a total game changer.

Now, let's talk about sprucing up both verbal and non-verbal communication. You might be asking, "How do I do that?" Here are some straightforward tips:

- Be patient. Some folks take a bit longer to get their thoughts out. Rushing them is like trying to microwave a frozen pizza—ain't gonna work.

- Use clear language. Ditch the idioms and jargon. Instead of saying, "It's raining cats and dogs," just say, "It's pouring." Easy peasy! Clarity is everything.

- Model communication. Show how to express thoughts and feelings. Use role-playing or storytelling to illustrate how it works in different situations. It's like teaching someone to ride a bike—they need to see it first!

- Practice active listening. Show you're tuned in. Nod, keep eye contact, and respond when needed. It's like a dance—both partners gotta be in sync.

Let's not overlook visual supports and aids. Visuals are like a GPS for communication, guiding folks through the maze of understanding. Here's why they're crucial:

- Clarity. Visual aids simplify complex info. Think of them as a map, showing the best route. Instead of getting lost in a word jungle, visuals give clear directions.

- Engagement. Visuals catch the eye. Ever tried slogging through a textbook with zero pictures? Snooze fest, right? Adding visuals makes things way more engaging.

- Memory aid. People remember images better than words. It's like recalling a movie scene vs. a script line—visuals stick!

So, how can you weave visual supports into your communication game? Check out these ideas:

- Use pictures. Create visual schedules or charts for daily activities. This helps folks know what's coming next, easing anxiety.

- Incorporate symbols. Use icons to represent feelings or actions. A happy face can show joy, while a sad face signals sadness. Simple but super effective!

- Leverage tech. Tons of apps and tools are out there to help with communication. From speech-generating devices to visual storytelling apps, tech can be your best buddy.

Now, you might be thinking, "What if this doesn't work?" Totally get that! Communication's a two-way street. It's all about trial and error. If one method flops, don't hesitate to switch gears and try something else. It's like shoe shopping—sometimes, you gotta try on a few pairs before you find the right fit.

And hey, don't forget to celebrate the little wins! Did someone nail a new communication method? Give 'em a high-five! Did they finally express a feeling they've been holding back? Throw a mini dance party! Positive vibes go a long way in boosting confidence and encouraging more communication.

As we wrap this up, let's take a sec to reflect. Communication challenges can feel overwhelming, but they're also a chance to grow. By understanding different communication styles, enhancing verbal and non-verbal cues, and using visual supports, we can create a more inclusive space for everyone.

Here's a little challenge for ya: try out one new strategy this week. Whether it's using visuals or honing your active listening skills, take that leap. You might find the world opens up in ways you didn't expect. Remember, it's all about progress, not perfection. Keep pushing forward, and soon enough, you'll be navigating the communication landscape like a pro!

Chapter 4

Let's jump into a topic that can feel as slippery as a greased pig at the county fair: social skills development. Seriously, this stuff can make or break your ability to connect with others. You might be asking, "Why's this even important?" Well, it's everything! Getting social cues and interactions down is like having a secret decoder ring for life—remember those from cereal boxes? Yeah, that's the ticket!

First up, social cues. These are the subtle signals that tell us what's happening in a convo or social scene. Think of 'em as the GPS of human interaction. They help steer us clear of awkward moments and keep us from driving into a metaphorical ditch. For folks on the autism spectrum, these cues can feel like they're written in a foreign language. I remember being a kid, feeling like everyone was speaking in riddles. I'd nod along, trying to figure it out while my brain screamed, "Can we just get to the point already?"

So, how do we teach these social skills effectively? Here are some techniques that can really make a difference:

1. **Modeling Behavior**: Show, don't just tell. This means acting out social situations in real life. Role-play things like ordering food or making small talk at a party. You'd be amazed how much easier it is to get a concept when you see it in action.

2. **Visual Supports**: Use visual aids to outline social scenarios. Flowcharts or comic strips can depict various interactions. This way, when your child or student faces a situation, they can refer back to these visuals for help. It's like having a cheat sheet for life!

3. **Social Stories**: Write personalized stories illustrating social situations. Include characters, settings, and outcomes that relate to the individual's experiences. It's storytelling with a purpose, and it can be a fun way to learn.

4. **Positive Reinforcement**: Celebrate every little success. Did they make eye contact during a convo? High five! Remember to ask a question instead of just rambling about their favorite dinosaur? Throw a mini party! Positive reinforcement can keep 'em motivated.

5. **Practice, Practice, Practice**: Like learning to ride a bike, mastering social skills takes practice. Set up playdates or group activities where they can interact with peers in a chill environment. The more they practice, the more confident they'll get.

Now, let's talk peer relationships and inclusion. This is where the magic happens! Friends provide a sense of belonging and support that's crucial for emotional well-being. It's like having your own personal cheer squad. But here's the kicker: inclusion isn't just about having friends; it's about creating a space where everyone feels welcome and valued.

Back in high school, I had a classmate who often got left out during group projects. It bummed me out because he had so much to offer. One day, I decided to include him in our group. You know what? It changed everything. He brought fresh ideas, and we learned a thing or two about resilience. Inclusion isn't just good for the individual; it enriches the whole group. So, let's dive into this!

Here are some strategies for building peer relationships and ensuring inclusion:

- **Encourage Group Activities**: Whether it's sports, clubs, or community events, get folks involved in group activities. These settings naturally promote interaction and help friendships bloom.

- **Educate Peers**: Teach classmates about autism and the importance of inclusion. Sometimes, all it takes is a little understanding to break down barriers. A simple classroom chat can work wonders for fostering empathy.

- **Create Buddy Systems**: Pair individuals on the spectrum with peers who can guide them through social situations. It's like having a personal social coach, easing the anxiety of new experiences.

- **Celebrate Differences**: Shine a light on each person's unique strengths. Whether it's a talent for art, math, or even trivia, celebrating these differences can boost confidence and help friendships grow.

- **Promote Open Communication**: Encourage open talks about feelings and experiences. When everyone feels safe to express themselves, it creates a supportive vibe that nurtures relationships.

So, what's the takeaway? Social skills are crucial, and they can be developed with the right techniques and support. Understanding social cues, using effective teaching methods, and fostering peer relationships can create a positive environment for growth. It's all about finding the right balance between guidance and independence. And trust me, when you see those social skills blossom, it's like watching a flower bloom in spring—absolutely beautiful!

Now, let's put this into action. Here's a quick challenge: Pick one social skill you wanna work on— maybe making eye contact or starting a convo. Create a plan using the techniques we discussed. Set a timeline, and don't forget to celebrate those little wins along the way! You got this!

In the end, social skills development is all about connection. It's about understanding, empathy, and building relationships that last a lifetime. So let's roll up our sleeves, get to work, and watch those social skills take flight!

Chapter 5

Behavior as Communication

Let's dive right into it, shall we? You know, when we think about behaviors—especially those that seem a bit, well, challenging—it's easy to throw our hands up in frustration. But here's the kicker: those behaviors are often just forms of expression. Think of it like this: if you were in a foreign country and couldn't find the right words to ask for help, wouldn't you start waving your arms and pointing at things? Exactly! That's what many individuals on the autism spectrum are doing when they exhibit challenging behaviors. They're trying to communicate something, even if it's not immediately clear to us.

So, what does this mean for us? It means we need to become behavior detectives. When a child is throwing a tantrum, it's not just a meltdown; it's a message wrapped in frustration. Maybe they're overwhelmed, tired, or just plain hungry. The trick is to step back and ask ourselves, "What's really going on here?" This perspective shift is HUGE. Instead of reacting with discipline, we can respond with understanding.

Now, let's talk about functional behavior assessments (FBAs). If you're scratching your head, don't worry—I was right there with you once. An FBA is like your roadmap for understanding behaviors. It helps us identify the "why" behind those actions. Think of it as the Sherlock Holmes of behavioral analysis. By observing the behavior, noting the context, and figuring out what happens before and after, we can uncover the motivations behind those actions.

For example, let's say you've got a kiddo who's constantly interrupting during class. An FBA would guide you to look at what's happening before they interrupt. Are they bored? Are they trying to get attention? By piecing together this puzzle, we can develop targeted strategies that address the root cause, rather than just the symptoms.

And speaking of strategies, let's dive into positive behavior support (PBS). This isn't just a fancy term; it's a game changer. PBS focuses on teaching new skills and encouraging positive behaviors rather than simply punishing negative ones. Imagine you're training a puppy. If you only scold it for chewing on your favorite shoes, it's not gonna learn what it should do instead. But if you reward it for playing with its toys, you're guiding it toward the right behavior. That's the essence of PBS.

Here's how to get started with PBS:

1. **Identify the behavior**: What's the specific behavior you want to change? Be as clear as possible.

2. **Understand the context**: What triggers the behavior? Is it a certain time of day, a specific location, or a particular activity?

3. **Teach alternative behaviors**: Instead of just saying "stop," show them what they can do instead. If they're yelling for attention, teach them to raise their hand or use a communication device.

4. **Reinforce positive behaviors**: Celebrate the small wins! When they use the new skill, give them a high five or a sticker. Positive reinforcement is like rocket fuel for behavior change.

5. **Monitor progress**: Keep track of how things are going. If something isn't working, don't be afraid to tweak your approach. Flexibility is key.

Now, I know what you might be thinking: "This sounds great, but what if it doesn't work?" Here's the thing—no single strategy is a magic bullet. Every individual is unique, and what works for one person might not work for another. That's why it's crucial to stay patient and keep experimenting. Think of it like trying on clothes; sometimes you have to sift through a few outfits before you find the perfect fit.

Let's take a moment to reflect on the impact of these strategies. Imagine a classroom where every child feels understood and supported. A place where challenging behaviors are seen as opportunities for growth rather than disruptions. It's like a well-tuned orchestra—each instrument playing its part, creating beautiful music together.

But here's the kicker: it starts with us. By interpreting behaviors as communication, conducting thorough functional behavior assessments, and implementing positive behavior support strategies, we're not just helping individuals on the spectrum. We're transforming our communities into more inclusive, understanding spaces.

So, what can you do right now?

- **Start observing**: Take a few days to watch the behaviors around you. What patterns do you notice?

- **Practice empathy**: When you see a challenging behavior, pause and ask yourself what message might be behind it.

- **Get educated**: Look into functional behavior assessments and positive behavior support strategies. There are tons of resources out there—books, online courses, and local workshops.

- **Share your insights**: Talk about what you've learned with others. The more we share, the more we can change perceptions and foster understanding.

Remember, you're not alone in this journey. We're all in this together, and every small step counts. Let's keep pushing forward, embracing the complexities of behavior, and striving for a world where every voice is heard, even when it's wrapped in a tantrum.

As we wrap up this section, keep in mind that behavior is a language all its own. By learning to interpret it, we open the door to deeper connections and more meaningful interactions. So, let's keep our detective hats on and continue this important work. After all, every behavior tells a story, and it's our job to listen.

Chapter 6

Sensory Sensitivities and Regulation

Let's dive into a topic that's near and dear to many of our hearts—SENSORY SENSITIVITIES. Now, if you've ever found yourself cringing at the sound of nails on a chalkboard or feeling overwhelmed in a crowded mall, you've got a taste of what many individuals on the autism spectrum experience daily. It's a wild ride, folks, and understanding these sensory triggers is key to making life a little smoother for everyone involved.

Identifying sensory triggers and their impact can feel like trying to find a needle in a haystack. But here's the thing: it's not impossible! Think of sensory triggers as those pesky little gremlins that sneak up on you when you least expect it. They can be anything from bright lights and loud noises to certain textures or even smells. For some, the smell of fresh popcorn can be delightful, while for others, it's like a slap in the face. It's all about the individual, and that's what makes it so crucial to pay attention.

So, how do we identify these triggers? Start by keeping a sensory journal. Yep, I said it—grab a notebook or open a notes app on your phone and jot down observations. Note when meltdowns or moments of discomfort happen. Was it a loud noise? A crowded space? A scratchy shirt? Over time, patterns will emerge. You'll start to see what sets off those gremlins, and that knowledge is POWER.

Now, let's talk about the impact of these triggers. When someone is overwhelmed by sensory input, it's like trying to drink from a fire hose—too much, too fast, and they're bound to drown. This can lead to anxiety, frustration, and even physical pain. It's a tough situation, and one that requires understanding and compassion from everyone around them.

But fear not! There are STRATEGIES for sensory regulation and coping mechanisms that can make a world of difference. First off, let's talk about the importance of having a toolkit. And no, I'm not talking about a literal toolbox filled with hammers and wrenches. I mean a sensory toolkit! This can include items like noise-canceling headphones, fidget toys, weighted blankets, or even a favorite scented lotion. The goal here is to have tools on hand that can help mitigate those overwhelming moments.

Another great strategy is to practice mindfulness and grounding techniques. Think of it like hitting the pause button on a chaotic scene in a movie. Deep breathing, counting to ten, or focusing on a specific object can help redirect attention and calm the nervous system. I once had a friend who swore by the "5-4-3-2-1" technique: name five things you can see, four things you can touch, three things you can hear, two things you can smell, and one thing you can taste. It's like a mini sensory scavenger hunt that brings you back to the present moment.

Now, let's not forget about the importance of creating sensory-friendly environments. Imagine walking into a room that feels like a warm hug instead of a chaotic circus. That's the goal! Here are some tips to make spaces more sensory-friendly:

1. **Lighting:** Soft, natural light is your best friend. Avoid fluorescent lights like they're the plague! If you can, use lamps with warm bulbs or even fairy lights for a cozy vibe.

2. **Sound:** Create a soundscape that promotes calm. Consider white noise machines or calming music. And for those moments when silence is golden, invest in some good noise-canceling headphones.

3. **Textures:** Be mindful of the materials in your space. Soft, plush fabrics can create a sense of comfort, while scratchy or stiff materials can be a sensory nightmare.

4. **Space:** Keep areas clutter-free. A tidy space can help reduce visual overload. Plus, it's easier to find what you need when you're not sifting through a mountain of stuff!

5. **Safe Zones:** Create a designated "safe space" where individuals can retreat when they need a break. This could be a cozy corner with pillows, a weighted blanket, or even a tent made of sheets.

Creating sensory-friendly environments isn't just about making things look nice; it's about fostering a sense of safety and comfort. It's about giving individuals the tools they need to thrive.

Now, I know what you're thinking: "This all sounds great, but how do I implement it in real life?" Here's a challenge for you—pick one sensory regulation strategy and one environmental change to implement this week. Maybe you'll start that sensory journal or rearrange your living room to create a cozy corner. Whatever it is, take that first step.

Remember, it's all about progress, not perfection. You're not going to create a sensory paradise overnight, and that's okay! Celebrate the small wins. If you notice a reduction in meltdowns or an increase in calm moments, that's a HUGE victory!

In the end, it's about understanding that sensory sensitivities are a part of the autism experience. They're not something to be fixed but rather embraced and accommodated. With a little awareness, some practical strategies, and a sprinkle of creativity, we can all work together to create a world that's a bit more sensory-friendly for everyone.

So, let's roll up our sleeves, put on our thinking caps, and tackle this sensory journey together. After all, we're all in this together, and every step counts!

Chapter 7

Educational Approaches and Strategies

Individualized Education Plans (IEPs) are the magic ingredient in the education system for kids on the autism spectrum. They're more than just forms; they're personalized guides crafted to fit each student's needs. Picture education as a pizza—an IEP is like the toppings that make it perfect for you. Want no pineapple? You got it!

So, what's inside an IEP? It includes key parts like goals, accommodations, and services. You start with present levels of performance, which tells you where the student currently stands. Next, there are annual goals—those are the targets we aim for over the year. Accommodations? Those are tweaks to the learning environment or teaching methods to help the student shine. Services might range from speech therapy to specialized instruction.

Let's get real for a sec. IEPs are only as effective as the folks behind them. It's not just about checking boxes; it's all about teamwork. Teachers, parents, and specialists need to join forces like the Avengers on a mission. Everyone brings something different to the table, and when they're in sync, it's a total game changer.

Speaking of game changers, let's dive into effective teaching methods. Not every kid learns the same way. It's like trying to shove a square peg into a round hole. We need to find the right fit. Here are some solid strategies to consider:

1. **Multi-Sensory Learning**: Engage different senses. Use visuals, sounds, and hands-on activities. This method caters to various learning styles and helps ideas stick like peanut butter.

2. **Structured Environment**: Kids with autism usually thrive in structured settings. Predictability is crucial. Use schedules and routines to create a safe space. It's like having a GPS for their day—no one likes getting lost!

3. **Positive Reinforcement**: Reward good behavior. It's like giving a high-five for a job well done. This can be as simple as verbal praise or little treats. Celebrate those wins, no matter how tiny.

4. **Visual Supports**: Use charts, diagrams, and visual schedules. These tools clarify expectations and make abstract ideas more tangible. Think of them as cheat codes for understanding.

5. **Flexible Grouping**: Mix it up! Sometimes, kids learn better in small groups or one-on-one. Being flexible helps cater to their social needs while boosting learning.

And let's not forget the importance of collaboration between educators and families. It's a two-way street, folks. Families know their kids inside and out. They're the real experts on their child's strengths, challenges, and triggers. When teachers and families team up, it creates a support network as solid as a rock.

Here's a little story for you. I had this student, Jake. His mom was a fierce advocate. She'd show up to every IEP meeting with insights about Jake's likes and dislikes. Together, we crafted an IEP that included his passion for dinosaurs. We turned math lessons into dino-themed adventures. Jake thrived, and honestly, it was a blast!

To make this collaboration work, here are some practical tips:

- **Open Communication**: Keep the conversation flowing. Regular check-ins keep everyone in the loop and allow for adjustments as needed.

- **Involve Families in Decision-Making**: Make them feel like part of the team. When families are involved, they're more likely to back the strategies at home.

- **Share Progress**: Celebrate successes together. When kids make strides, let everyone know! A quick email or call can build trust.

- **Provide Resources**: Give families tools and strategies they can use at home. It's like handing them a toolbox for success.

Now, you might be thinking, "That's all well and good, but how do I actually put this into practice?" Let's break it down into actionable steps.

1. **Get Familiar with IEPs**: If you're a parent or educator, take the time to learn about IEPs. Know what's included and how to advocate for your child or student.

2. **Assess Learning Styles**: Observe how the child learns best. Are they visual? Kinesthetic? Tailor your teaching methods accordingly.

3. **Create a Structured Environment**: Set up a consistent routine at school or home. Use visual schedules to guide the day.

4. **Foster Collaboration**: Schedule regular meetings with families to discuss progress and strategies. Make it a partnership, not a one-way street.

5. **Be Flexible**: Be open to changing methods as needed. What works today might not work tomorrow, and that's totally okay!

6. **Celebrate Small Wins**: Keep the momentum going by celebrating progress, no matter how small. It builds confidence and motivation.

7. **Seek Feedback**: Don't hesitate to ask for input from families and other educators. They might have valuable insights to enhance the learning experience.

At the end of the day, the goal is to create an educational experience as unique as each child. There's no one-size-fits-all here. It's all about finding what clicks for each individual.

So, whether you're a parent, teacher, or just someone looking to make a difference, embrace the journey. It might get bumpy at times, but with the right strategies and a whole lot of heart, you can help kids on the autism spectrum grow and thrive. Let's roll up our sleeves and get to work—every child deserves a shot at shining bright!

Chapter 8

Family Dynamics and Support

Navigating the world of family relationships can feel like trying to walk a tightrope while juggling flaming torches—challenging, nerve-wracking, and, let's be honest, a little ridiculous at times. When you throw autism into the mix, it can feel like you've suddenly added a trampoline to the equation. But don't worry! With the right strategies and support, you can find your balance and even have a little fun along the way.

Let's dive into how to navigate these family dynamics. First off, every family is unique. You've got your own quirks, your own history, and your own way of doing things. But one thing is universal: the need for open communication. If you're not talking, you're not connecting. And connection is key, especially when supporting a loved one on the autism spectrum.

Start by having family meetings. I know, I know—sounds about as exciting as watching paint dry, right? But hear me out. These meetings can be a safe space for everyone to share their thoughts and feelings. You might even want to throw in some snacks to sweeten the deal! Encourage each family member to voice their concerns, joys, and questions. Make it a judgment-free zone. This way, everyone feels heard and valued.

Now, here's a little tip: use "I" statements. Instead of saying, "You never listen to me," try, "I feel unheard when we don't talk about our experiences." It's like putting a cherry on top of a sundae—it makes the conversation more palatable and less confrontational.

Next up, let's talk about resources and support networks. You're not alone in this journey, folks! There are countless organizations and online communities that offer a wealth of information and support. Websites like Autism Speaks and the Autism Society provide resources ranging from educational materials to local support groups. Seriously, it's like having a treasure map that leads you to gold nuggets of wisdom!

Consider joining a local support group. Meeting other families who are navigating similar challenges can be a game-changer. You'll find camaraderie, shared experiences, and maybe even a few laughs along the way. Trust me, you'll leave those meetings feeling like you just had a heart-to-heart with a good friend.

And speaking of friends, don't forget about your own social circle. Your pals can be a great source of support too. Whether it's venting over coffee or getting together for a fun night out, maintaining those friendships is crucial for your well-being.

Now, let's shift gears and talk about self-care strategies for caregivers. If you're feeling drained, you can't pour from an empty cup. So, how do you fill that cup? Here are some practical tips to get you started:

1. Prioritize "me time." Whether it's reading a book, taking a long bath, or binge-watching your favorite show, carve out time just for you. Think of it as a mini-vacation for your soul.

2. Get moving! Exercise is a fantastic way to relieve stress. Even a brisk walk around the block can do wonders for your mood. Just remember to wear comfy shoes—your feet will thank you.

3. Connect with other caregivers. Share your experiences, swap stories, and laugh about the

craziness of it all. You might even find that you have more in common than you think!

4. Practice mindfulness. Take a few minutes each day to breathe deeply and focus on the present moment. It's like hitting the reset button on your brain.

5. Seek professional help if you need it. There's no shame in talking to a therapist or counselor. They can provide valuable insights and coping strategies tailored to your unique situation.

As you navigate the ups and downs of family dynamics, remember to celebrate the small victories. Maybe your child said a new word, or perhaps you finally had a calm family dinner. Whatever it is, acknowledge it! These little moments add up and remind you that progress is happening, even when it feels slow.

In the end, supporting a loved one with autism is a team effort. It takes patience, understanding, and a whole lot of love. So, gather your family, share your thoughts, lean on your support networks, and don't forget to take care of yourself. After all, you're the backbone of this journey, and you deserve all the support you can get.

Now, go ahead and tackle those family dynamics with confidence! You've got this!

Chapter 9

Fostering Independence

When we talk about fostering independence, we're diving into some pretty crucial waters. It's not just about teaching someone how to make a sandwich or tie their shoes—though, trust me, those are essential skills. It's about giving individuals the tools they need to navigate life with confidence and autonomy. So, let's break this down into bite-sized pieces, shall we?

First off, let's chat about daily living skills and routines. Think of these as the bread and butter of independence. If you've ever tried to cook a meal without knowing how to boil water, you know how important these skills are. Daily living skills encompass everything from personal hygiene to managing finances. It's like equipping someone with a Swiss Army knife for life.

Now, here's a fun fact: Research shows that teaching daily living skills can significantly boost self-esteem and reduce anxiety. Who doesn't want that? When individuals learn to manage their own routines, they gain a sense of control over their environment. And let's face it, feeling in control is like finding that last slice of pizza at a party—pure gold.

So, how do we go about teaching these skills? Here's a handy list to get you started:

1. **Break It Down**: Start with small, manageable tasks. Instead of saying, "Let's clean the house," try, "Let's pick up all the toys in the living room."

2. **Use Visual Aids**: Create charts or checklists. Visual supports are like GPS for daily tasks—super helpful in navigating the chaos.

3. **Practice, Practice, Practice**: Repetition is key. The more you practice, the more second nature these tasks become. Just like riding a bike— eventually, you won't even think about it!

4. **Celebrate Successes**: No matter how small, celebrate those victories. Did they make their bed?

Awesome! Give a high-five and maybe a sticker. Positive reinforcement goes a long way.

Now, let's pivot to the importance of choice and autonomy. This is where things get really interesting. Imagine you're at a restaurant, and the waiter asks what you'd like to order. If you say, "I'll have whatever," you might end up with something you absolutely hate. That's what it feels like when individuals don't have a say in their lives. Choices are like the seasoning in your favorite dish—without them, everything feels bland.

Giving individuals the power to make choices helps them develop critical thinking skills. It's like teaching someone to fish instead of just giving them a fish. When they make choices, they learn to weigh options, consider consequences, and ultimately take ownership of their decisions.

Here are some practical ways to encourage choice and autonomy:

- **Offer Options**: Instead of saying, "Do you want to go to the store?" try, "Would you like to go to the store or stay home and read?" This simple shift opens the door for choice.

- **Respect Their Decisions**: Even if you think they're making the wrong choice, let them choose. It's their life, after all! Remember, sometimes the best lessons come from making mistakes.

- **Encourage Self-Advocacy**: Teach individuals to express their preferences. Role-playing can be a fun way to practice this. For instance, simulate a scenario where they have to advocate for their favorite activity.

Now, let's talk transitions—specifically, preparing for transitions into adulthood. This is where the rubber meets the road. Transitioning into adulthood can feel like jumping off a diving board into the deep end. It's exciting, but it can also be terrifying. The key here is preparation.

Research indicates that individuals who receive proper transition planning are more likely to succeed in adulthood. We're talking higher employment rates, better social skills, and increased independence. It's like having a roadmap before embarking on a cross-country road trip.

Here's how to get the ball rolling on those transitions:

1. **Start Early**: Don't wait until the last minute. Begin discussing future goals and aspirations in early adolescence. It's like planting a seed—give it time to grow.

2. **Create a Transition Plan**: This plan should outline goals, necessary skills, and steps to achieve those goals. Think of it as a game plan for the big leagues.

3. **Involve the Individual**: This is their life, so their input is crucial. Ask them what they want to achieve and how they envision their future.

4. **Provide Resources**: Connect them with job training programs, vocational rehabilitation services, or mentorship opportunities. These resources can be game-changers.

5. **Practice Life Skills**: As they approach adulthood, focus on skills like budgeting, cooking, and job interviewing. These are the tools they'll need to thrive.

Remember, the goal is to help individuals feel empowered and equipped to tackle adulthood head-on. It's like giving them a superhero cape—suddenly, they can soar!

As we wrap this up, I want you to take a moment and reflect. How can you implement these strategies in your own life or the life of someone you care about? What steps can you take today to foster independence?

In the end, fostering independence isn't just about teaching skills; it's about creating opportunities for growth and self-discovery. It's about celebrating every little victory along the way. So, roll up your sleeves, grab that metaphorical toolbox, and get to work. You've got this!

Chapter 10

Emotional Regulation and Mental Health

Understanding emotional dysregulation in autism? Man, it's like trying to catch smoke—slippery and overwhelming. But let's break it down. Emotional dysregulation means struggling to manage emotional responses. For folks on the autism spectrum, this can lead to intense reactions over small stuff. Imagine a kid spills juice at lunch, and instead of just being a bit upset, it's like the world's ending! It's not about being dramatic; their emotional responses are just heightened.

So, what's cooking in that brain of theirs? Well, neurodiverse brains process emotions differently. It's like watching a movie in high-def while everyone else is stuck with black-and-white. This can spark feelings of anxiety, frustration, or anger when things go off the rails. And let's be real—life throws curveballs, and not all of 'em are fun.

Now, let's tackle the big stuff: anxiety and depression. These two often crash the party uninvited, dragging a ton of baggage. Studies show folks with autism are more likely to face anxiety and depression. Seriously, about 40% of people on the spectrum might deal with anxiety at some point. That's a big number! So, how do we handle this?

First, let's focus on emotional well-being. You're probably wondering, "How?" Let's hit you with some techniques that can really help.

Mindfulness and Breathing: Teach deep breathing. It's like hitting the reset button. When anxiety creeps in, take a moment. Breathe in for four counts, hold for four, breathe out for four. Repeat until you're feeling chill.

Routine and Structure: Having a routine gives a sense of security. It's like a roadmap for the day. When things go off-script, it's unsettling. So, keep it predictable!

Emotion Regulation Skills: Help folks identify and label their emotions. Use visuals or charts. It's like giving them a toolbox for their feelings. "I'm feeling frustrated" is way easier than "I'm feeling everything at once!"

Physical Activity: Get moving! Dance it out in the living room or take a stroll in the park. Physical activity helps release pent-up emotions. Think of it as letting off steam before a pressure cooker explodes.

Creative Outlets: Art, music, writing—these are powerful ways to express feelings. Sometimes, words just don't cut it, but a paintbrush or guitar can say a lot.

And let's not forget support systems. Surrounding individuals with understanding friends and family? Huge! It's like having a safety net. When things get tough, knowing there are people who "get it" is comforting.

Now, you might be thinking, "What about professional help?" Great question! Therapy can be a game-changer. Cognitive Behavioral Therapy (CBT) can help folks reframe negative thoughts and develop coping strategies. It's like having a personal trainer for your mind.

But here's the kicker: mental health isn't just about fixing problems; it's about nurturing strengths. Many individuals with autism have unique talents and perspectives. Celebrate those! Encourage them to chase their passions. This boosts self-esteem and creates a sense of belonging.

Incorporating these strategies into daily life? It might feel like learning a new dance. At first, you might trip over your feet, but with practice, you'll find your groove. Start small—maybe introduce one new technique each week. Before you know it, you'll be gliding through life with a bit more grace.

Let's take a sec to reflect. Ever felt overwhelmed by emotions? Had a day where everything went wrong, and you just wanted to hide under the covers? We all have those days! It's key to remember that emotional dysregulation is part of being human, not just something that hits those with autism.

So here's a challenge: Next time emotions bubble up, pause and take a breath. Ask yourself, "What's really going on here?" This simple act of reflection can help you understand your feelings better and respond more effectively.

To wrap it up, emotional regulation and mental health are super important for individuals with autism. By grasping emotional dysregulation, promoting well-being, and tackling anxiety and depression, we can create a supportive environment that fosters growth.

Remember, it's not about being perfect; it's about making progress. Every little step counts. So let's keep moving forward, one breath at a time! And if you ever feel lost, just know: you're not alone. We're all navigating this wild ride together, finding our way to emotional well-being.

Chapter 11

Therapeutic Interventions

When it comes to supporting individuals on the autism spectrum, therapy can feel like a buffet—so many options, and you're not sure what's gonna hit the spot. From Applied Behavior Analysis (ABA) to Occupational Therapy (OT) to Speech Therapy, each type of intervention offers unique flavors and benefits. So, how do you pick the right one? And once you've chosen, how do you know if it's working? Grab a snack and let's dive into this.

First off, let's break down these therapies. ABA is like that Swiss Army knife of interventions—it's versatile and widely used. It focuses on reinforcing positive behaviors while reducing challenging ones. Think of it as teaching skills through a system of rewards. When my cousin started ABA, he learned to express his needs rather than throwing a tantrum. It was a game changer for his family.

Then there's Occupational Therapy, which is all about helping individuals develop the skills needed for daily living. OT is like the superhero of independence. Whether it's buttoning a shirt or navigating a crowded room, OTs help individuals tackle life's challenges head-on. I remember watching my friend's son, who struggled with sensory sensitivities, learn to use tools for self-regulation during his OT sessions. It was inspiring to see him transform from overwhelmed to empowered.

Speech Therapy is equally crucial, especially for those who may struggle with communication. This therapy helps improve both verbal and non-verbal communication skills. It's like giving someone the keys to a locked door—they can finally express themselves! I've seen kids who were once non-verbal find their voices through speech therapy, and it's a beautiful thing.

Now, you might be wondering, "How do I choose the right therapy for my loved one?" That's a million-dollar question, and it's not one-size-fits-all. Here are some practical steps to guide you:

1. **Assess Individual Needs**: Start by evaluating the specific challenges your loved one faces. Is it communication? Daily living skills? Social interactions? Knowing the primary focus will help narrow down your options.

2. **Consult Professionals**: Don't hesitate to seek advice from specialists—doctors, psychologists, or therapists can provide valuable insights tailored to your situation. They can help you understand which therapy aligns best with your loved one's needs.

3. **Consider Personal Preferences**: Just like you wouldn't force a kid to eat broccoli if they prefer pizza, it's essential to consider what your loved one enjoys. Engaging in a therapy they find fun and motivating can lead to better outcomes.

4. **Explore Options**: Look into local providers and programs. Many offer introductory sessions, so you can test the waters before diving in. This is like sampling before you buy; you want to ensure it's a good fit.

5. **Trust Your Gut**: At the end of the day, you know your loved one best. If something feels off, or if they're not responding well to a particular therapy, don't be afraid to pivot. Flexibility is key.

Now, let's talk about measuring the effectiveness of these therapeutic interventions. It's not just about feeling good; it's about seeing real, tangible progress. Here's how you can keep tabs on what's working and what's not:

1. **Set Clear Goals**: Before starting any therapy, establish specific, measurable goals. This could be as simple as "increase communication attempts" or "improve social interactions." Having clear targets gives you a benchmark to measure against.

2. **Track Progress Regularly**: Keep a journal or log of your loved one's progress. Note any changes in behavior, communication, or skills. This can help you identify patterns and celebrate victories—no matter how small.

3. **Use Data**: Many therapists use data collection methods to track progress. If your therapist isn't already doing this, ask them to incorporate it. Numbers can provide a clear picture of improvement and help guide future interventions.

4. **Solicit Feedback**: Regularly check in with the therapists. They can provide insights on what's working and what might need adjusting. Collaboration is crucial—think of it as a team effort.

5. **Be Patient**: Change doesn't happen overnight. It's like planting a seed; you won't see the flowers immediately, but with time and care, they'll

bloom. Celebrate the small steps along the way, and don't get discouraged if progress feels slow.

Let's be real for a second: navigating the world of therapeutic interventions can be overwhelming. But remember, you're not alone in this journey. Surround yourself with a support network—other parents, professionals, and community resources. Share experiences, swap stories, and lean on each other. There's strength in numbers, and together, you can tackle any challenge.

As you embark on this adventure, keep in mind that each individual is unique. What works for one person may not work for another, and that's okay. Embrace the journey, trust the process, and don't forget to celebrate the wins—no matter how small. After all, progress is progress, and every step forward is a reason to cheer.

In conclusion, choosing the right therapeutic intervention is like finding the perfect pair of shoes. It may take some time, a bit of trial and error, but when you find that fit, it makes all the difference. So, get out there, explore your options, and don't hesitate to make adjustments along the way. Your loved one deserves the best support possible, and with the right tools, they can thrive. Keep pushing forward, and remember: YOU'VE GOT THIS!

Chapter 12

The Role of Technology

Let's chat about tech, okay? It's everywhere and shaking things up for folks on the autism spectrum. Remember when flip phones were all the rage? Now we've got smartphones and tablets that can do just about anything—except maybe cook dinner. If you find a gadget that can whip up a lasagna, hit me up!

First off, let's get into assistive tech and communication devices. These bad boys are like magic for many individuals with autism. They help make communication smoother, turning what could be a frustrating mess into something manageable. Imagine a kid who struggles to share their thoughts suddenly getting a tablet loaded with a communication app. With a few taps, they can express their feelings and needs. It's like giving them a voice when words are tough to come by.

So, what kind of devices are we talking about? Here's the lowdown:

1. Speech-Generating Devices (SGDs): These handy gadgets can produce speech. They range from simple devices that speak pre-set phrases to advanced software that lets users customize their communication. Picture a kiddo using an SGD to order their fave pizza—talk about feeling empowered!

2. Augmentative and Alternative Communication (AAC) Apps: These apps are made for smartphones and tablets, featuring symbols and pictures users can tap to create sentences. It's like building sentences with Legos, but way cooler.

3. Text-to-Speech Tools: These tools read text aloud, a total game-changer for those who find reading a struggle. It's like having a personal assistant ready to help out.

Now, let's shift gears and talk about apps for social skills and learning. There's an app for just about everything these days, and social skills training is no different. Interacting with others can be tough, especially for those on the spectrum. But don't sweat it! With the right tools, learning these skills can be less intimidating.

Check out some popular apps and tools:

- Social Stories: These apps help create personalized stories outlining social situations. Think of them as roadmaps for tricky social landscapes, covering everything from greetings to personal space.

- Role-Playing Games: Yup, you read that right! Some apps use role-playing scenarios to teach social skills. It's like a fun game of "let's pretend," but with a purpose. Users can practice responding to social cues in a safe space.

- Video Modeling: This method uses videos to show proper social interactions. It's like watching a YouTube tutorial, but instead of baking a cake, you're learning how to make friends.

So, what's the takeaway? Tech isn't just a tool; it's a lifeline for many individuals with autism. It's about finding what fits each person's unique needs. Like hunting for the perfect pair of jeans, it might take some trial and error, but it's totally worth it.

Now, let's get a bit futuristic and chat about virtual reality (VR) in therapy. This is where it gets really exciting! VR can create immersive experiences tailored to individual needs. Imagine practicing social skills in a virtual café or a crowded park without the sensory overload of the real world. It's like a training ground for real-life situations.

Here's how VR can make a difference:

1. Safe Environment: VR lets individuals practice social interactions in a controlled space. They can learn to navigate conversations, respond to social cues, and handle unexpected situations—all without real-life pressure.

2. Sensory Regulation: For those sensitive to sensory input, VR can be adjusted for a comfy experience. Users can tweak volume, lighting, and other sensory aspects to their liking. It's like having a personal sensory paradise!

3. Motivation and Engagement: Let's be real— kids love tech. VR can make learning fun and engaging. When therapy feels like a game, folks are more likely to participate and remember what they learn.

Now, you might be thinking, "This all sounds awesome, but how do I get started?" Here are some practical steps to weave tech into your approach:

- Research Available Tools: Take some time to explore the latest assistive technologies and apps. Websites like the Assistive Technology Industry Association (ATIA) and the Center on Technology and Disability (CTD) are solid resources.

- Trial and Error: Don't hesitate to try different devices and apps. What works for one person might not for another. It's all about finding the right match.

- Involve the Individual: If possible, get the person with autism involved in the decision-making. Let them check out different tools and see what clicks. After all, they're the ones using it!

- Seek Professional Guidance: If you're feeling lost, consider chatting with a speech-language pathologist or occupational therapist. They can offer insights and recommendations tailored to individual needs.

- Stay Informed: Tech is always changing, so keep up with the latest trends and tools. Join online forums or groups to share experiences and learn from others.

In conclusion, technology is a powerful ally for individuals on the autism spectrum. From assistive devices to VR therapy, the possibilities are endless. Embrace this tech revolution and watch it open doors to communication, learning, and social skills. Remember, the goal is to empower individuals to thrive, and tech can play a key role in that journey.

So, are you ready to jump into the world of technology? It's time to explore, experiment, and embrace the tools that can make a real difference. Let's get started!

Chapter 13

Advocacy and Awareness

Self-advocacy. It's a big word, but it's got a simple meaning: speaking up for yourself. When it comes to autism, it's not just important—it's ESSENTIAL. I mean, who knows you better than you, right? Think of it this way: if you don't advocate for yourself, who will? It's like going to a restaurant and letting the waiter decide your meal. You wouldn't do that! You've got to take charge and make your preferences known. Empowerment isn't just a buzzword; it's your ticket to a life where you feel heard and respected.

Now, I get it. Advocating for yourself can feel daunting. You might think, "What if they don't listen?" or "What if I mess it up?" But here's the kicker: self-advocacy is a skill, and like any skill, it gets easier with practice. Start small. Maybe it's asking for a specific accommodation at school or work. Maybe it's simply sharing your needs with friends or family. Each time you speak up, you're building that muscle, flexing your voice a little more. And trust me, it'll pay off in spades.

Let's chat about some strategies for advocating within your community. Community is everything, folks. It's where we connect, learn, and grow. So, how do you become a voice in your community? Here are a few ideas to get you started:

1. **Get Involved**: Join local advocacy groups or organizations that focus on autism awareness. You'll meet people who share your passion and can help amplify your voice. Plus, it's a great way to make friends!

2. **Educate Others**: Host workshops or information sessions. You don't have to be a PhD to share what you know. Use your experiences to educate others about autism. You'd be surprised how many misconceptions are out there.

3. **Share Your Story**: There's power in storytelling. Share your journey—what it's like to live with autism, the challenges you face, and the victories you celebrate. People connect with stories; it makes the information relatable.

4. **Leverage Social Media**: Use platforms like Facebook, Instagram, or TikTok to spread awareness. Share articles, create posts, or even start a blog. The internet is a powerful tool for advocacy. Use it!

5. **Engage with Local Leaders**: Reach out to local officials or community leaders. Invite them to events or ask them to support autism-friendly initiatives. Remember, they're there to serve the community—make your voice heard!

Now, let's dive into raising awareness and reducing stigma. This is where the rubber meets the road, folks. Stigma can be a heavy weight to carry, but together, we can lighten that load. The first step is education. Did you know that a whopping 70% of people believe they understand autism, but only 30% can accurately define it? That's a massive gap! By educating ourselves and others, we can bridge that divide.

Here's how to tackle stigma head-on:

- **Start Conversations**: Don't shy away from discussions about autism. Talk about it openly. The more we normalize these conversations, the less stigma will exist.

- **Challenge Stereotypes**: If you hear someone making an offhand comment or perpetuating a stereotype, speak up! It might feel uncomfortable, but it's crucial. Change starts with YOU.

- **Celebrate Differences**: Instead of viewing autism as a deficit, let's celebrate the unique perspectives and talents that come with it. Share success stories, highlight strengths, and show the world that different is beautiful.

- **Advocate for Inclusive Policies**: Work with local schools, businesses, and organizations to create policies that promote inclusion and understanding. The more inclusive our environments, the less stigma we'll see.

- **Use Humor Wisely**: Humor can be a powerful tool. It can break down barriers and foster connection. Just make sure it's respectful and doesn't punch down. A good laugh can make tough conversations easier.

And hey, let's not forget the importance of self-care in advocacy. You can't pour from an empty cup, right? Make sure you're taking care of yourself while you're out there advocating for others. Set boundaries, take breaks, and celebrate your wins—no matter how small they may seem.

In my own journey, I remember a time when I felt like a lone wolf. I was frustrated, unsure of how to advocate for myself. But once I found my community, everything changed. I joined a local support group, and suddenly, I wasn't alone anymore. We shared tips, strategies, and stories that made me feel empowered. I learned that advocacy doesn't have to be a solo mission; it's a team sport!

So, what's the takeaway here? Advocacy and awareness are about more than just speaking up; they're about building a community, fostering understanding, and creating a world where everyone feels valued. Whether you're advocating for yourself or someone else, remember: your voice matters. You have the power to make a difference.

Now, I challenge you. Take one of these strategies and put it into action this week. Whether it's sharing your story on social media or reaching out to a local leader, just do it! The world needs your voice, and it's time to let it shine.

Chapter 14

Let's dive into something that really fires me up: recognizing and nurturing individual strengths. Seriously, everyone's got something special to bring to the table. Remember that saying, "You can't judge a fish by its ability to climb a tree"? It's spot on. Each of us has unique talents that deserve to shine, especially for folks on the autism spectrum, where these strengths can be truly remarkable.

First off, let's be clear—autism isn't a cookie-cutter label. It's a spectrum, kinda like a box of crayons, all different colors and shades. Some people can memorize facts like it's nobody's business, while others create mind-blowing art or music. The key? Recognizing these strengths is the first step to nurturing them.

Think about it. Ever met someone who lights up when they talk about what they love? That energy is infectious, right? That's what we wanna cultivate. So, how do we make that happen?

First, listen and observe. Seriously, just take a step back and watch. What gets them excited? What makes them smile? It's not just about their skills; it's about what brings them joy.

Next, encourage exploration. Let them try new stuff! Sign them up for a pottery class, a coding boot camp, or even a local theater group. You never know what hidden talent might pop up.

And don't forget to celebrate the small wins. Did they finish a project? Create something cool? Celebrate it! A simple "Wow, that's awesome!" can boost their confidence more than you'd think.

Now, let's sprinkle in some success stories. I once met this guy, Jake, at a community event. He was pretty quiet at first, but when he started talking about his love for robotics, his face lit up like a Christmas tree. He built his own robot from scratch—no kidding! With a little nudge and support, he entered a local competition and—drumroll, please—won first place!

Jake's not alone. There are tons of folks on the spectrum who've turned their passions into real successes. Whether it's an artist whose work is in galleries or a tech genius making apps, these stories remind us how powerful it is to recognize and nurture strengths.

Now, let's switch gears and chat about creating opportunities for skill development. It's not just about spotting strengths; it's about building on them. Think of it like planting a seed. You can't just toss it in the ground and forget about it. You gotta water it, give it sunlight, and maybe even chat with it a bit. (Who doesn't love a good pep talk, right?)

Here's how to create those opportunities:

Connect with local resources. Many communities have programs to help individuals on the spectrum develop their skills. Look for workshops, classes, or mentorship programs.

Set goals together. Work with the individual to establish realistic, achievable goals. Whether it's learning something new or finishing a project, having a clear target can be a huge motivator.

Provide constructive feedback. This is crucial. Instead of pointing out what didn't work, focus on what did. "I loved how you tackled that problem! Let's tweak this part together."

Foster a growth mindset. Encourage the belief that abilities can grow with dedication and effort. This mindset can change the game.

Now, you might be thinking, "What if they're not into anything?" I get it. It can be a struggle to find that spark. But here's a tip: try different things without the pressure of commitment. It's like a buffet—sample a little of everything until you find what you dig.

Remember, the goal isn't to force a passion but to create a safe space for exploration.

To wrap it up, celebrating strengths and talents is more than just recognition; it's about taking action. Here's what you can do right now:

Make a list. Sit down with the individual and jot down their strengths. Don't hold back—go all in!

Plan a fun activity. Whether it's a trip to a museum or a DIY craft day at home, plan something that aligns with their interests.

Share success stories. Find stories of others who've succeeded. It can be super inspiring and motivating.

Be patient. Growth takes time. Celebrate the journey, not just the destination.

So, there you have it! Celebrating strengths and talents isn't just a nice idea; it's crucial for supporting individuals on the autism spectrum. By recognizing what makes them unique, sharing success stories, and creating opportunities for skill development, we can help them shine brighter than a supernova.

And let's be real—who doesn't wanna be part of a world where everyone gets to strut their stuff? So get out there, roll up your sleeves, and start celebrating those strengths! You might just uncover a hidden talent in yourself along the way.

Chapter 15

Creating a Supportive Community

Building an inclusive community for folks on the autism spectrum is super important. Think of it like a big, warm hug on a cold day—comforting and essential. A solid community can help bridge gaps, foster understanding, and form relationships that make everyone feel welcome. But how do we whip up this kind of community? Let's break it down.

First, why does community matter? Here's a little story for ya. A while back, I volunteered at an autism support group. One night, a mom opened up about feeling totally alone. She was struggling to raise her child on the spectrum, and it felt like no one got it. Fast forward a few months, and she started making connections. She found friends who understood her struggles, shared tips, and offered support. That's the beauty of community—creating spaces where folks feel safe and understood.

So, how do we get that sense of belonging going? One way is by teaming up with local organizations. If you're thinking, "Where do I even start?" no sweat! Here's a quick checklist to kick things off:

1. **Find local groups**: Look for autism advocacy organizations, schools, or community centers focused on inclusion. They usually have programs and resources ready to roll.

2. **Reach out**: Don't hold back! Give them a call or shoot an email. Ask about partnerships, volunteer gigs, or events. You'd be amazed at how many people are ready to jump in.

3. **Host events**: Plan community get-togethers, workshops, or info sessions. Make it fun! A potluck, movie night, or game day can really bring folks together.

4. **Share resources**: Put together a community resource guide listing local services, support groups, and activities. Get it out there through schools, libraries, and social media. The more info people have, the better they can support each other.

5. **Encourage involvement**: Invite families, educators, and individuals on the spectrum to join discussions. Their voices are crucial, and including them strengthens the community.

Now, let's switch gears and talk about building a culture of acceptance and understanding. This is where the rubber meets the road. It's not just about having a community; it's about creating an environment where everyone feels valued. Here's how to do that:

- **Education is key**: Host workshops or seminars to teach the community about autism. Bring in speakers, share personal stories, and bust some myths. The more folks know, the less fear and stigma there'll be.

- **Promote empathy**: Encourage everyone to step into the shoes of individuals on the spectrum. Share stories, create empathy-building activities, and foster connections. It's all about understanding, not just tolerating.

- **Celebrate diversity**: Shine a light on the unique strengths and talents of individuals on the spectrum. Organize events showcasing their skills— art shows, talent nights, or science fairs. When people see the beauty in diversity, acceptance follows.

- **Lead by example**: If you want a culture of acceptance, you gotta model it. Be the change you wanna see! Show kindness, understanding, and support to everyone around you. Your actions will inspire others.

- **Create safe spaces**: Make sure community spaces are welcoming and accommodating. This could mean sensory-friendly environments, quiet areas, or resources for those who need them. Everyone should feel like they belong.

And let's not forget the magic of storytelling. Sharing personal experiences can be super powerful. I once met a young guy named Jake at a community event. He was on the spectrum and loved music. During an open mic night, he shared his journey through song. His heartfelt lyrics hit home for everyone in the room. It was a beautiful reminder that we all have stories worth sharing, and those stories can build connection and understanding.

Now you might be asking, "This all sounds great, but how do I actually start?" Here's a quick action plan to help you build that supportive community:

1. **Assess your community**: Look around. What resources are already there? What gaps need filling? This'll give you a clearer picture of what you're working with.

2. **Engage with local leaders**: Connect with schools, local government, and community organizations. They can be powerful allies in your mission.

3. **Create a community calendar**: List events, workshops, and gatherings related to autism and inclusion. Share it widely so everyone knows what's up.

4. **Utilize social media**: Set up a Facebook group or Instagram page for your community efforts. It's a great way to spread the word, share resources, and keep everyone in the loop.

5. **Gather feedback**: Regularly check in with community members. What's working? What's not? Their input will help you refine your approach and ensure you're meeting everyone's needs.

Building a supportive community takes time and effort, but the rewards are huge. You're not just creating a network; you're building relationships that can change lives. And who knows? You might just find your own sense of belonging along the way.

So, let's wrap this up with a little pep talk. You've got this! Whether you're a parent, educator, or just a community member, you have the power to make a difference. It's all about taking that first step—no matter how small. So grab your metaphorical shovel, dig in, and start building that supportive community. Together, we can create a world where everyone is included, accepted, and celebrated for who they are. Now, go out there and make some magic happen!